T0158997

BIGFOOT:
Believe It or Not

DON EDGERS

authorHOUSE®

AuthorHouse™
1663 Liberty Drive
Bloomington, IN 47403
www.authorhouse.com
Phone: 1 (800) 839-8640

© *2018 Don Edgers. All rights reserved.*

No part of this book may be reproduced, stored in a retrieval system, or
transmitted by any means without the written permission of the author.

Published by AuthorHouse 09/12/2018

ISBN: 978-1-5462-5932-9 (sc)
ISBN: 978-1-5462-5933-6 (e)

Print information available on the last page.

Any people depicted in stock imagery provided by Getty Images are models,
and such images are being used for illustrative purposes only.
Certain stock imagery © Getty Images.

This book is printed on acid-free paper.

Because of the dynamic nature of the Internet, any web addresses or links contained in
this book may have changed since publication and may no longer be valid. The views
expressed in this work are solely those of the author and do not necessarily reflect the
views of the publisher, and the publisher hereby disclaims any responsibility for them.

Contents

Acknowledgements

Special thanks to my wife, Carolyn, who patiently and tirelessly read, corrected, and encouraged me while composing this book. My daughter, Eryn, introduced me to the realm of Bigfoot and allowed me to accompany her into the Olympic and Cascade Mountains and Forests. My grandson, Phoenix Raye, kept me on task and put up with my snoring only a few feet from his head. As a retired educator, I discovered and learned of an area of knowledge about which I knew nothing – all this while keeping physically fit. Son-in-law, Mark "Jax" Jackson, was of great assistance in formatting this book into its present form.

Bigfoot Research Organization (BFRO), Washington Bigfoot Research (WABFR) [An unofficial group], The Olympic Project, and offshoot groups from the aforementioned are all to be acknowledged for their positive contributions to responsibly maintaining our forests and mountains.

Kudos to Col. Kevin Jones (ret.) (BFRO), Scott Taylor (BFRO), Ric Hjertberg (BFRO), Tyler Bounds (BFRO), Derek Randles (The Olympic Project) who are all constructively involved in the search and reporting of all things Bigfoot.

Thanks to my long-time friend John Mikkelborg for his painting titled "BF Puzzle." This painting was displayed (NFS) along with non BF paintings for sale at exhibitions in Arizona.

Those who contributed their writings to be included in this book are Laura Roeder, Nate Helgeson, Michael Beers and Eryn Jackson.

The cover design is by Alicia Bateman

Thanks to photographer Cindy Rose Caddell for permission to use BFRO group picture - 2012

I want to thank some of those who, not mentioned above, made my campouts enjoyable and memorable, such as: Bob Gimlin (Bigfoot legend/godfather), Dave G [archeologist] (whom I would pay [but didn't] to show up in camp to tell his stories), Nate H, Ghee B, Rayn M, Darrel V, Peter S, Ted C, Denise -, Geoff R, Barb O, Maryellen, Renae, Johnny B, John H III (RN), et al.

~ 1 ~

Who's Who?

The identity of the three-generations of Bigfoot "investigators" whose adventures are related in this book:

[1st Generation – dad] ~ *Don Edgers*: Retired high school teacher (30 years), U.S. Army veteran, organic gardener, world traveler, lives in a woodsy area of Kitsap County (WA) called McCormick Woods.

Because I've authored articles and books (none related to Bigfoot) and have a daughter, Eryn, who's into Bigfoot *bigtime* and chronicled many of her BF experiences, I thought we should blend our tales, plus my grandson, Phoenix's, into this book.

I've been a camper, like sleeping on the ground in a sleeping bag, from early childhood, plus as a Cub and Boy Scout, and U.S. Army soldier (call me crazy) enjoyed roughing it outdoors.

[2nd Generation – daughter/mom] ~ *Eryn J.*: Retired horse farmer/ trainer/breeder, ADVENTURER, and International artist who sells artwork online and in-person at conventions for Sasquatch and paranormal. Her shop is called 'Feral by Eryn'. She has camped outdoors since childhood and lives on 5-acres, mostly wooded.

[3rd Generation- grandson]~ *Phoenix R*: College student, athlete, intrepid explorer. He lived in or around woods his entire life, and is always up for a walk in forests to see what he can discover.

People want to know why Eryn and I don't take our spouses:

Don's wife, Carolyn, isn't interested in being uncomfortable – she's been there & done that, but appreciates that dad, daughter and grandson can do something together while she does things she enjoys doing in the comfort of home.

Eryn's husband, Jax, is a city-raised Scotsman and finds it rather difficult to go camping in a kilt. He understands Eryn's hobby and the fact that the three intrepid "Bigfooters" spend time together while he works around their property and takes care of their domestic animals.

Phoenix, Eryn and Don (author) prepared to Squatch

~ 2 ~

BF Doubters, Distractors & Hoaxers

When I began Bigfoot treks and told my neighbors, friends or acquaintances I was going Squatching (BF hunting), the majority of them smiled slyly, rolled their eyes, or if they were drinking something – blow the liquid out their nose (you can't laugh and swallow at the same time). Other folks seemed to be happy to see me go. And then there was an occasional snarky well-wisher who said something like, "If you catch one, tag it and release it, 'cuz we don't want it in our neighborhood."

Now, I roll with the jibes, and ignore the so-called "expert" opinions of those who've made up their mind on hearsay or what they say is lack of evidence, like armchair BF hunters who have watched Bigfoot shows wonder why they never see one.

There are the occasional folks, aka 'Outdoor Bigfoot Hackers', who get a kick out of fooling or making fun of Bigfooters who are seriously looking for BF, like Mike Dodge (*The Legend of Mike Dodge*) who's known as "the Barefoot Sensei" and hangs out in the area of the Hoh Rain Forest of the Olympic Mountains. He makes and leaves fake BF footprints, and returns calls of BF howlers when they're in his neck of the woods.

When we're near public campgrounds, unhappy campers will sometimes return our howls with their howls, honk their car horns, or get on our walkie-talkie frequency spouting obscenities.

Then there are the all-out hoaxers who make a supreme effort to disprove the existence of Bigfoot by using their thumb-to-nose meanness by creating realistic fake BF prints. After creating a trail of prints, like in the mud of a receding lake, the hoaxer will call a BFRO researcher to leave a tip. The researcher will check out the tip, and if the prints look convincing, alert others who make casts. The BF casters take photos, make casts and display them at Bigfoot gatherings. The first time I saw hoaxed-prints, I actually got excited. The detail was what I considered *perfect*. After Bigfoot researchers made a big whoop-de-do about the prints and casts, the informant/tipster called to let them know he created the prints (lol?).

Some hoaxers create realistic Bigfoot costumes and arrange to have photos or videos made, then claim because they made up their images, all other videos and pictures are more than likely fake. There's even one person claiming credit for dressing up as the BF in the Patterson/Gimlin 1967 16mm film footage. The problem is, his costume is of a male Bigfoot; the film is of a female.

In 1958 a construction worker in a Northern California logging camp found 16" humanlike footprints that got the attention of the *Humboldt Times* which used the term *Bigfoot* for the first time. Supposedly, according to relatives, a man named Ray Wallace carved wooden feet and strapped them onto his boots to make the impressions. The *New York Times*, when Ray passed away in 2002, declared in a front-page story that "Ray Wallace was the hoaxer behind Bigfoot." The fact is that the size and shape of the wood feet didn't match the size or shape of the casts made of the prints.

In 2012, Randy Lee Tenley, a Montana man trying to create a Bigfoot hoax by dressing in a *Ghillie suit* (camouflage-type clothing designed to look like heavy foliage), stepped out onto a highway and was killed after being hit by two cars.

The attempted debunking of Bigfoot takes more than raising doubts through deception, hearsay or rumors. If you concentrate on armchair–nonparticipating Bigfoot sceptics, don't pass judgement on those who believe. As the TV show *The X-Files* tagline says, "The Truth Is Out There." **Believe it or NOT!**

BF Puzzle
By John Mikkelborg

~ 3 ~

What's in a name?

Bigfoot - Sasquatch

Q. What do you call a cross between a gorilla and parrot?
A. I don't know, but when it talks I listen.

This begs the question of what to call a bipedal, large hairy creature that lives in the woods, looks like a man/gorilla, makes human/animal-type noises in the night and has large feet?

Among the descriptive names given to this entity are: ape-man; man-monkey; monkey-man; big hairy monster; hairy (ones, giants, people), etc. The Salish Native People of British Columbia used the word se'sxac ('Wild*man*') which English speakers pronounce 'Sasquatch' (ca. 1920s). From all of these names, primarily Sasquatch and Bigfoot (ca. 1960s) survive and are used interchangeably. When I go on a Bigfoot campout, I don't say, "I'm going out to search for Bigfoot," instead I say, "I'm going Squatching."

Examining the moniker 'Bigfoot' is cherry picking from the various descriptive features of this uncommon, reclusive, large, hairy hominoid which lives year-round off the beaten path in the forests and mountains. It is also described as a *cryptid* which is defined as a living thing having the quality of being hidden or unknown.

UNCOMMON

This title puts BF in a category of 'rarely seen or encountered'. Although, because of TV shows and internet exposure to the subject, many reported wilderness experiences of hunters, campers or people living near wooded areas, audio/visual contact is more prevalent than previously reported. Also, many folks who experienced encounters and were embarrassed to admit it are speaking up at Town Meetings or online sites.

RECLUSIVE

'As *reclusive* as a Melungeon' is a somewhat-applicable tag line. Who or what are Melungeons? They are described as tri-racial isolates who lived in isolated communities in the central Appalachian Mountains in parts of Tennessee, Virginia and Kentucky. Bigfoot can't claim to be that reclusive because of the large number of Bigfoot sightings reported in mountainous and forested areas especially of northwestern United States and British Columbia, Canada. Judging from the reports, BF doesn't want to integrate with our society, and only watches us from sheltered areas, getting a closer look in the dark. Basically, we're engaging in Bigfoot hide and seek – and we're "it" most of the time.

LARGE

By *large* we're talking tall and husky, like *really BIG*. Canadian Eduard Beaupré, aka 'the Willow Bunch Giant', who upon his death in 1902, was 8'2.5", weighing over 400#. Andre the Giant (wrestler and actor) at 7'4", weighed in at 475#. The tallest person in recorded history, Robert Wadlow (1918-1940), aka, "The Alton (IL) Giant" was 8'11", weighing 439#. (Weights and heights vary in various reports – the point being – they're LARGE!)

Gigantism is seemingly caused by an overactive pituitary gland and might be passed on genetically through a mutated gene.

HAIRY

Hairy is a predominate descriptor of BF, which leads to those who claim to see the creature to think it may be related to apes or monkeys. Medical science calls excessive hairiness in humans: *hirsutism, hypertrichosis* or *polytrichosis* and is caused by genetics (DNA). It may also be caused by an abnormality of endocrine glands, pituitary or adrenal glands. Women who suffer Polycystic Ovary Syndrome have excessive body hair. There are many records of hairy men and women throughout recorded history. As early as 1850 B.C. the Bible relates the birth of fraternal twins Esau and Jacob. Esau (which means 'hairy') was born covered in red hair. So-called (hairy) "freaks-of-nature" are written about and pictured in the 19th and 20th century, with *some* of these humans being displayed in circus and "freak" shows.

From 1962-1964 I was stationed, courtesy of the U.S. Army, in Northern Japan on the island of Hokkaido. There were two dining room personnel in the mess hall who were noticeably not Japanese. I discovered they were descendants of an ethnic group known as Ainus (eye-news). These indigenous people were the original inhabitants of this northern area of Japan and parts of Russia. A physical characteristic is hairiness. In an Ainu museum in Sapporo (famous for their beer), there are many skulls showing the physical difference between Japanese and Ainu. Japanese skulls resemble our Native Americans, i.e., Indians. Ainu skulls resemble Caucasian skulls.

HOMONOID

Omnivorous mammals of the Order *hominoid* are classified as *primates,* which includes humans and some of the great apes, i.e., erect bipedal primate mammals. The Bigfoot in the 1967 Patterson-Gimlin film shows a walking Bigfoot female.

NOISY

Yells, howls, whistles, wood knocks, clacking rocks, and even "talk" have all been heard and recorded frequently on Bigfoot outings. The best recordings were made by Ron Morehead who wrote *Voice in the Wilderness* (with Thom Powell); *Quantum BIGFOOT*. Morehead made these recordings titled *the Sierra Sounds* in the 1970s while on a hunting trip in a remote area of the California part of the Sierra Nevada Mountains.

Eryn (daughter) and Phoenix (grandson) heard a squabbling-sounding youthful BF in 2012 in the Cascade Mountains near Morton, Washington. Phoenix also saw it @ 20 feet. Also, very loud whistles were heard not far away (others in the vicinity also heard the whistles).

I've heard howls in the distance and "talk" near my tent. The so-called talk sounded like a foreign language conversation between two different males (because of the different voice pitch). Others who've heard this "talking" label it *Samurai Chatter*. Linguist and experienced foreign language analyst, R. Scott Nelson, says it is actual intelligent conversation in an undocumented language.

The object of our human howls is to elicit a response from any BF in our vicinity. While on a campout with other Bigfooters near Nisqually Pass in the Cascades, Laura, who has a beautiful singing voice, let out with an operatic-sounding version of the theme song for *Star Trek*. When she was finished, we all heard multiple howls from ----- coyotes. They approved.

BIG FEET

Dr. Jeff Meldrum, Ph.D., professor of Anatomy & Anthropology at Idaho State University and author of *From Biped to Strider*, and *Sasquatch: Legend Meets Science*. In 2013 he published a *Sasquatch Field Guide* which unequivocally differentiates animal, human and Sasquatch foot prints. Meldrum came across 15" bare foot prints that weren't animal (bear) or human. My grandson wears size 15 shoes, and when wandering in the woods and mountains doesn't go barefooted. If he did, his prints would be easily identified as human. The point of speaking about barefoot prints in the *wilderness* is why would any sane person go shoeless in remote and rough locations?

FINAL ANSWER

At the beginning of this topic I asked, "What do you call a bipedal, large hairy creature that lives in the woods, looks like a man/gorilla, makes human/animal-type noises and has large feet?"
ANSWER – ***BIGFOOT.***

SPECULATIONS

There are those much more qualified than me in the field of biology, primatology, anthropology, etc. who seem to think Bigfoot/Sasquatch are possibly mostly apes. Book titles like *Sasquatch: The Apes Among Us* by John Green and *North America's Great Ape: the SASQUATCH* by wildlife biologist John A. Bindernagel, PhD.

Others, often armchair-analysts, think a 'cross-between-species' theory is a possibility, i.e. human and ape.

Finally, there is the school of thought in the paranormal-thinking 'camp' that supposes there is an alien (as in other-worldly) connection. This point of view is clearly presented in Thom Powell's book *Edges of Science.*

~ 4 ~

Why Do People Search for Bigfoot?

What's That Sound?

When I was a boy, my summers were spent on Fox Island in South Puget Sound. Most days were spent fishing or exploring the shoreline from my rowboat.

One early evening as I was rowing around a 13-acre island which had been an Indian graveyard in the olden days, and was located in a bay near my house, I heard what sounded like a woman cry for help. I rowed toward the sound in the hopes that I could see a 'damsel in distress.' I heard the cry a couple of more times and shouted out, "Where are you?" with no response. I quickly rowed home to report what I had heard, whereupon one of my older brothers, who was a counselor for a boys camp located on the little island, informed me that what I had heard was a peacock, they had brought there. Roosters crow, ducks quack – peacocks yell 'help.' And so it did for many years. I never saw the bird except once when it flew from its island to our island and stood beside the road as I was driving to work.

I relate this story to illustrate why some people search for the source of husky sounding yowls, screams, whistles, wood knocks or other unaccounted-for sounds coming from the woods.

My daughter and grandson drove up to the Morton BFRO Expedition area a week after the event so he could see where the campout that he couldn't attend took place. They stopped on a logging road, and immediately heard a racket that, as Eryn describes it, "sounded like a pig squealing under water." Phoenix piped up with, "I'll bet it's a Bigfoot," and jumped out of the Jeep and headed toward the commotion. Because we'd been told not to run toward BF, Eryn shouted at him to come back. Thirteen-year-old's choose not to always follow directions, so the young wanna-be Squatch hunter continued around a bend and came upon the source of the sound, only about 20 feet from a young BF which continued to squall while shaking a bush at the interloper who dared to enter into his domain. Phoenix yelled back to his mother, "Mom, it's right here, a little one, and it's so clean!" (Meaning - there were no leaves or forest dander clinging to its shiny light brown fur). It reminded him of *Chaka* from the TV show *Land of the Lost*. Afterwards, he referred to it as his *Chaka* sighting. When Phoenix looked back, the critter smacked two trees with its hands as a warning, got down on all fours, scrambling through tall underbrush towards the sounds of loud human-sounding whistles. Eryn was too far back to see the creature, but saw the brush being parted as it retreated, and heard the loud whistles.

Besides *searching for the sources* of curious sounds, there remain a plethora (bunch) of **other reasons** to hike into wilderness settings, like:

- Hunters who've spotted a large hairy humanlike creature while looking for game animals. Several Bigfooters have had this experience, and in one case the observation continued for over 30 minutes. These experiences have more or less primed the pump of the curious to get a closer look at creatures seen at a distance. This is a version of forestland hide and seek.
- Bucket list fulfillment. Interestingly, over the course of several BF outings I've come in contact with individuals who want to have an outdoor experience with a reported large hairy creature that lives in the woods. These folks have come from several states (Southeast, Midwest, etc.) and even from a foreign country, not counting Canada.
- Camping with a purpose (John R.). Some BF campers simply like to camp with others for the outdoor experience of "hunting" in a secure setting. It's like safety in numbers in case of emergency or perhaps a wild animal invasion. The location of BF camps is selected because of multiple reports of sightings or other typical sights and sounds attributed to BF. If it looks like a Bigfoot, sounds like a Bigfoot, smells like a Bigfoot ------
- In order to demonstrate their personalities, Bigfooters exhibit behaviors applicable to those of their ilk. There are different **Personality Behavior Theories** that might explain those who make up Camp Bigfoot.

    1. _Type A_ – More driven, outgoing, impatient, ambitious, focused, bossy, competitive, walk fast & with a purpose, love problem solving, etc. (Paul Hudson)
       Type B – Laid back, relaxed, enjoy the moment, "enjoyment of the game" (BF Camping?) (*Psychology Today*)

    2. _Meyers-Briggs 16 Personality Types_
       Four Categories and their characteristics
       Analysts – Architect, logician, commander, debater
       Diplomats – Advocate, mediator, protagonist, campaigner
       Sentinels – Logician, defender, executive, consul
       Explorers – Virtuoso, adventurer, entertainer, entrepreneur

Personally, as a Type B, Adventurer, my theory is that all types are represented in the Bigfooters mix; some exhibiting stronger behaviors in one or more area than others. At one time in my university studies I came across some psychology professors and authors who demonstrated what Ronald Reagan to have said, "It's not that they're ignorant, it's just that they know so much about what isn't so."

- People who have Bigfoot/Sasquatch phobia sometimes appear at BF campouts, seeming to want to face their fears. At one BF outing, there were three people wearing side arms – which, to me, looked as out of place as a clothed person at a nudist camp. I asked one of the least threatening looking pistol-packer why he carried a pistol. He had *three reasons.* The *first* was because a relative of his who worked in a logging camp, told of an incident when he returned to the camp one evening and came upon a Bigfoot (hairy and large) which walked ahead of his vehicle and then into the woods. This relative developed a mantra of 'If you ever see a Bigfoot – shoot it!' This Bigfoot encounter was repeated over the course of several years.

The *second* reason was because his dad took him to see *The Legend of Boggy Creek,* a horror film featuring a Bigfoot-type monster. After being scared witless, and on the way home in the dark, his dad made a turn up a wooded lane, slowly decreased speed, then drifted backward (because of taking the car out of gear) and exclaimed, "Bigfoot's pulling us back!" After Bigfoot "released" the car, and father and child made it back home, the child had the horror of Bigfoot burned into his soul and sought safety under his bed.

The *third* reason happened in the recent past after his home had been built at the end of a road in the woods. Several nighttime incidents occurred where his home would be slapped by something and got to the point that a rifle was kept by the door for protection against BF intrusion. One late afternoon, a man who had been clearing brush and making a burn pile a little way down a bank from the "slapped house", informed the pistol-packer, there was a Bigfoot by the pile. The homeowner grabbed his rifle, got the BF in his sight and found that he was unable to squeeze the trigger.

- Curiosity seekers want to have the experience of being in the midst of those who profess to have actually seen this human-like hairy creature inhabiting the woods.

- In the case of Lee and Anita Townsend, with whom I've done Bigfoot camping, they have come from two different "camps" in that Lee has been interested in BF since 1968 when he read an article in *Argosy* magazine by Ivan T. Sanderson, a Scottish biologist and writer who wrote 34 books ranging from classic nature writing to paranormal subjects. He coined the word *cryptozoology* which is defined as the study of hidden animals. Lee then got more interested in 2002 when he read a book by Sanderson about how Bigfoot meets science. In 2006 he went on a BFRO Expedition and camped in the Cascade Mountains by a lake with many of the Who's Who in the current Bigfoot world. Lee and Anita continued attending BF outings and Town Meetings where Bigfoot was the topic. On their way home after a 2012 Town Hall meeting in Payson, Arizona, Anita saw a BF on the edge of CA SR 1. This eventually led to other sightings (as close as 10-feet) which she has written about in a 2017 booklet: *Anita's Sasquatch Sightings and Background*. There are some interesting pictures and drawings.

- Spending a few days in wilderness areas with likeminded campers, free from the demands of daily hubbub and where clean air can be breathed while getting good exercise seem to be reasons enough to go on a Bigfoot Trek. And it's possible to see the Milky Way at night!

~ 5 ~

In the Beginning

Qualifications & Observations.:

If anybody tells me they've seen or done something out of the ordinary, no matter what I might think about the situation, I believe them, unless I can factually prove them wrong. To actually see, hear and/ or experience something is completely different from just hearing or reading about it; such as *Carnival* in Rio de Janeiro, Brazil. My wife and I had heard about it and seen pictures and videos of it, but to experience it as we did in 2017 was amazingly different. The same can be said of other experiences like mountain climbing, deep-sea diving, Bigfoot hunting, etc. Not participating in an activity and actually getting involved are two different experiences.

As a septuagenarian (in my seventies) I've seen and visited many places in the world, like Japan (26 months), Egypt, Spain, India, Greece, South America, etc. Even though my visits to various places were around the world, I'd never spent much time in the forests and mountains located only hours away from my home in Washington State.

Until 2012 I didn't really concern myself with sightings of Bigfoot/ Sasquatch, After all, there were similar reports of Elvis sightings. I really didn't care about the "sightings" of either one; whereas my daughter, Eryn, developed such an interest (because she believed she saw a BF when she was younger on a trip into the Cascade Mountains) when she read about an upcoming Big Foot Research Organization (BFRO) outing, and went through a vetting application in order to qualify to attend. That done, she had to plunk down $300 and have someone else to go along with her. Possible camping partners she asked to go with her couldn't go for various reasons (they were probably thinking, 'you're going to do WHAT!?') so Dad got selected. After I was checked-out and approved, we set about gathering suggested supplies, clothing and equipment for our first of several BF gatherings.

Our expedition was slated for May somewhere in Washington's Cascade Mountains. Campers were advised on what camping supplies and equipment to bring, and what scenario to expect. Our camping experience obviously wasn't going to be haphazard.

<u>Heads up to readers</u>: The following reports have various people's names mentioned throughout. I have chosen to use first names for those who either haven't given me permission, or haven't had their full names mentioned on public websites. It will become evident who were active in our searches in various locations. Some locations aren't specifically named in order to keep looky-loos from visiting BF hotspots.

~ 6 ~

BF Expedition #1

May 17-20, 2012

Only Eryn & I were on our first Bigfoot outing, because Phoenix, much to his chagrin, was still in school.

We drove to Morton, WA, a logging town and Bigfoot (BF) sighting hot spot near Mt. St. Helens in the Cascade Mountains. We followed "confidential "directions to one particular logging road which was one of many that permeate the mountain forests.

Precautions were taken in order that possible interlopers don't get involved with BF activities. At our first contact point outside of the base camp we were met by a Bigfooter named Su, who sort of appeared from behind a tree and some bushes. She told us to set our walkie-talkies (cell phone reception isn't an option) to a designated frequency and proceed ahead as she called to alert those already in the camp that we were coming.

As we arrived at our destination, its initial appearance aroused within me the feeling I got when landing on a sparsely inhabited island in the South Seas. It seemed like all activity stopped and the campers froze in place. All eyes were on us, and a couple of men in well-used camping attire approached to find out who we were, and directed us to possible camping areas where we could set up our tents to unload everything but our food. After we were settled we returned to base camp.

There were so many campers, aka "Bigfooters," on this expedition (over 75) that camping spots were set up at various places near the base camp and up to ½ mile away. Eryn & I set up our tents about a ¼ mile away with an experienced Bigfooter named John R, in a spot used by deer hunters (judging by trash, targets, and remnants of camp fires.)

The base camp was a large dug or blasted-out rock quarry where the blasted chunks of rock were ground into gravel for logging roads. This particular quarry resembled the shape of a two-sided rock-walled amphitheater with the level area allowing space for six or more tents, toilet tent, and a cover to shelter a table of maps and several casts of BF foot impressions. There also was a trailer with supplies and gear used by the BF organizers.

After setting up camp we carried our foldup camp chairs to base camp where those who were able to arrive on Thursday gathered. We were introduced to the expedition leaders: Col. Kevin Jones (Ret.), Ric, Kurt and their helpers: Tyler, John R and Su as well as other seasoned "Squatchers": Rayn, Scott, Lee, Anita, et al.

It seems that whenever a group of strangers get together everyone sizes up each other. This group consisted of relatively normal-looking individuals of various sizes and ages with more males than females.

We newcomers introduced ourselves, and got instructions of what to listen and look for and after splitting up into three or four groups, set out on a night walk. The group I was in stopped at a place that divided into two roads, and while stopped by a gate to one road we heard a howl that didn't sound like a coyote or a wolf, but rather like a person who stepped on a rusty nail. (I say this from experience) Each of us decided to duck under the bar of the gate blocking the road in order to head in the howl's direction. I discovered I'm not good at ducking under road gates, probably because I was wearing clunky boots, and I'm a bit hampered in coordination because of a stroke. Anyway, I bit the gravel and was kindly lifted up by two nurses, Maryellen and Renae.

After a cold and uncomfortable night with the loud sounds of snoring from the tent next door, we heated up water for coffee to have with our energy bars for breakfast, and headed to the main camp to watch and meet our fellow campers and listen to any overnight experiences. Nothing major transpired so we were briefed on our surroundings and told what we might listen or watch for in the forest around us that might be BF related. More campers would be coming to join us throughout the day and we were on our own until we all gathered in late afternoon.

Not satisfied with our morning eats, a trip to town for commercial coffee, food, snacks and ice, we headed out to a nearby logging town to fill up our larders and stomachs with civilized foodstuff. We were greeted with the sight of some of our fellow tribesmen at a gas station/market and Subway whom had similar appetites and explanations of, "Since we were filling up our gas tanks, we thought we'd check out the market."

Back at camp, our group was setting up wherever a spot could be found. When most of them were settled we gathered with our chairs circled around a fire pit. Everyone was introduced. Most attendees were from various part of Washington State and Oregon. There was one family of four and a smattering of couples, and many "Lone Rangers." The walks-of-life represented were students, IT programmers for various companies, nurses, business owners, a masseuse, etc. Ages were from early teens to mid-seventies.

Daytime activities were things like casting footprints, signs or indications of BF, areas and plants to avoid, using walkie-talkies on the "frequency of the day", first aid, and survival situations. A couple in my age category, Lee & Anita, went for a walk on a game trail, and when they returned found a tree pushed over the trail. They cut off one of the branches with a crook in it to make a walking stick for me to help steady my gait. (Even now, years later, I continue to use it on my almost-daily walks in my neck of the woods.)

The second night Eryn and six other "girls" decided to spend the night at an outpost area they called Camp 7, near an abandoned homestead that had the remnants of an apple orchard. It's believed by veteran Bigfooters that BF is attracted to females and children, AKA, "bait", so this would be a test of the 'female' part of the theory. The ladies separated into night-walk groups, and one group heard what they believed was something tracking them in the woods next to them. To test their suspicion they would suddenly stop and then hear something take a step after they'd stop. Another group reported seeing what looked like red eyes looking at them from behind a tree. It was a moonless night, so the light was not reflected from any existing light source. Bigfoot paranoia ---?

The seven ladies set up three tents around a fire with Eryn & Rayn placing their tent further away from the others. Eryn had brought several glow sticks with a different color for each lady. She chose to use a blue-colored one to put into a pocket inside her tent. The blue light was visible through the tent's fabric from the outside. Eryn, lay awake from the excitement of a BF outing while the other six campmates slept soundly because of exhaustion. About 2 AM there was the sound of what sounded like duff or needles hitting the side of the tent in the area of the glow stick near her head. Remaining still, the next sound was what sounded like pebbles or sticks striking the same area. When the sound of a loud crack outside alarmed her, Eryn grabbed her tent-mate to find out if she'd heard the noises. She hadn't and soon drifted back to sleep.

Later, as Eryn became drowsy the sound of what sounded like drumsticks tapping in rhythm and in four different locations kept her alert. A while later, with her eyes shut, she sensed the light from the glow stick varying in intensity and upon opening her eyes the glow stick seemed to get right next to her head, like something had pushed it into her face, so she pushed back and the contest ended. All was silent for a while, when pine cones and sticks were periodically thrown at the light. About 4 AM it began to get light and all activity ceased. Evidently this was BF's first encounter and reaction to a new element it couldn't figure out.

Eryn, still pumped from her experiences, never really got any sleep, so with the dawn's early light she hiked up to the road where her Jeep was in order to light her stove and brew coffee. The other ladies of camp were still in their tents sawing logs, so when she heard someone call her name, she asked who wanted her. There was no response, and when she returned to camp, everybody was still asleep. When all were awake, no one claimed to have called her name. Hmmm…

Camping cuisine – I'm not a picky eater, so I was interested in what experienced BFROers eat. John R. is a died-in-the-wool MRE (meals ready to eat) aficionado. I also saw another MREer mixing and squishing his MRE packet, then spooning the goo into his mouth. After tasting the concoction the partakers seemed to check the label to see what it was supposed to be, shrug their shoulders, and take another bite or gulp. In a Charlie Chaplin film called "*The Gold Rush*" there's a scene where Charlie and another prospector are reduced to eating candles and one of Charlie's stewed boots. He starts by rolling up the rawhide boot laces and eating it like spaghetti while the other miner looks at him like he's crazy. Well – – – – I suspect MREs are meat flavored powdered sponges – or something. I preferred Col. Kevin's choice of cuisine: early big breakfast at a restaurant in town a few miles away, and Nalley's chili spooned right from the can for lunch or dinner. Eryn and I ate a couple of meals at a Subway in town, but mainly subsisted on ramen, premade meals, fruit and energy bars.

I thoroughly enjoyed the day and night-walks and sharing around the fire pit at Base Camp. While toasting marshmallows one night, Kevin shared an experience of a camper whose marshmallow caught on fire and rather than blow out the flame, waved it up and down vigorously causing the flaming mallow to fly off the fork and land on his tent. It managed to burn a hole through the tent, and narrowly missed his sleeping bag.

Possible Bigfoot calling cards appeared on our musical night walk and a day walk by Lee & Anita. The signs were freshly pushed over trees (roots and all). Lee & Anita's tree was done within a ten minute period. They sawed off a walking stick-sized chunk of the tree and presented it to me as a stabilizer in my wood walks. It's a nice reminder of my BFRO experience.

Another reminder of my experience is a 24" hematoma, extending from my hip to my knee. Coincidentally, it looks much like a Bigfoot imprint. At the end of a night walk on the first night, people were ducking under a metal road block gate. I was wearing my clunky cold-weather boots and when I ducked under caught my boot on a rock, which threw me off balance and I crashed onto that big chunky gravel used on logging roads, landing on my elbow and hip. Thanks go to Maryellen and Renae (nurses) for help in raising me up.

Even though I can scratch the BFRO Expedition off my bucket list, I'll go on another one with the hope of seeing glowing eyes, and maybe get a whiff that defies description.

~ 7 ~

BF Expedition 2

June 12-16, 2012

This expedition took place three weeks after the Morton BFRO outing with a smaller group calling itself Washington Big Foot Research Organization (WABFR) and in a different location: a lake next to Chinook Pass in Eastern Washington.

This location is open to the public with camping areas located in the forest between mountainous terrain and a lake, and a BF hotspot. It is reached by traversing Chinook Pass in the Cascade Mountains which had recently been opened after being cleared of snow. In fact it was snowing lightly as we crossed. Patches of snow were throughout the lower elevation in the area of our campsites.

Opening day of Chinook Pass

The reason this BF outing took place when it did was because not many public campers would be around and any resident Squatches (BF) might be in the vicinity. Also, it was an opportunity for those who wanted to use the information and limited experience gleaned from the recent BFRO Expedition to practice what we had learned.

Most of our group set up in an area called "Rock Camp" because of its proximity to piles of large rocks which have sloughed off mountain cliffs only 150-or-so yards away.

Other campsites nearby are named California Camp, Frog Camp, Dog Camp, Spooky Camp, and Twilight Zone – all named for various reasons related to many previous BF outings.

We BF newbies got to meet some BF old-timers who weren't present at our recent expedition and hear about their experiences at this location. One of them, Ted C, brought his dog with him, which was something that wasn't allowed at the Morton outing. Beta, an aged German shepherd, was no problem and fairly comfortable and friendly with our group.

I was reminded of a camping experience my wife and I had when camping on the Oregon coast with our dog, Jeater. We'd been on the road about three days, stopping at public campgrounds at night and driving and walking on the ocean beaches during the day. We were doing fine until the afternoon we pulled into Humbug Mountain State Park. We had established a routine of finding a campsite first and then heading for the beach.

At Humbug a sign was posted that we hadn't seen anywhere else, saying: "All dogs must be on a leash!" No doubt violators would be tied to a stake and burned alive, so I improvised a leash out of a 25 foot section of clothesline and took off on a trek to the beach. With our trusty canine tugging at the clothesline, we worked our way past tents and campers. I noticed that one camper had two large German shepherds chained to it, and when they caught sight of us coming past them, they lit up like they suddenly had a reason to live. They both started barking madly and tugging at their chains as our mutt trotted toward them to make friends. Time seemed to stop and I looked in horror as first, one snarling dog broke loose and then the other. I pulled our dog back to me as far as possible, but the two police dogs were gaining so fast on what they thought was dinner on a rope that, with ten feet to go, I had to swing our dog around my head to keep the attacking dogs from mutilating him. Fortunately, the collar on our pup held as did the knot I tied, as I continued swinging the dog in a circle while yelling for help. Every time the dog passed over the heads of the others, they'd jump and try to bite it. I don't know if there is a record in the *Guinness Book of World Records* for the longest time for a dog swung over a person's head at the end of a rope, but if there is, Jeater should be number one.

After about a minute, which seemed like a lifetime, the owners of the other dogs showed up and dragged them away, and I was able to land our poor dog. He rolled about three times. Several people had gathered around thinking what they had seen was part of a campground show, and when my dog landed, they broke into applause. Okay, okay, there wasn't any applause; however, everything else happened. The dog lived for several more years and was never leashed again.

Meanwhile, back at the BF Camp, Ted had a camper-tent that he shared with Beta. The camper had a kitchen, of sorts, which was used to cook up some pretty tasty victuals, like the Cajun dish, Jambalaya. I'll eat just about anything that's a switch from ramen, even though I love it, and Ted's dish was worth two helpings. The Colonel brought *two* pressure cookers and lots of potatoes, carrots, onions and about 5# of steak to cook up as a stew to feed us hungry Bigfooters (for two or three days?). On just about every BF outing, somebody would come up with something special to satisfy our stomachs.

Every night we split into groups to explore various roads or paths in the hope that we'd experience the presence of a BF. It was thought that if we let out whoops or hollers we'd let the objects of our hunt be aware of our location and/or get an audio response. One evening at twilight we had a six-year-old girl in our midst when we stopped, and Scott (the best hollerer of all time) let out a howl that made the tree tops tremble, and scared the tar out of the little girl. She latched onto one of my fingers so hard that I thought *I* might also let out with a howl. I asked her if she wanted to go back to camp, and not releasing my finger, she agreed to the proposition. It's thought that BF is attracted to children, not to eat, but because kids don't have a threatening attitude.

The second night Kevin, Su and I went down the road for about ½ mile, then detoured into a deep woods trail that meandered toward the area to a camp near a swamp which had been the sight of a BF that ran through the area and was seen by several campers. I have very good night vision, but didn't have my headlamp with the recommended red lens, so was stumbling at the rear over the unlit uneven terrain at a slower (cougar-bait) pace when I decided to stay where I was until the fast-walkers returned. Waiting in the moonless night, I could only hear my ears ring and my heartbeat. About 20 minutes later, when I surmised Su and Kevin were hopelessly lost or snatched and eaten by forest cannibals, I heard the faint sound of voices. I had been standing on the trail, leaning on a tree, so stepped back into the bushes next to the trail and waited until I could see the hikers, then stepped out to join them. Su was so startled she let out a scream. A second or so later I thought I heard a reply coming from the woods.

Eryn and Laura claimed to have had an 'eye glow' experience. Eye glow is when the eyes of a creature (in this case a BF) emanate light (usually red) that is not reflected from another light source – such as the moon or flashlight. What's known as 'eye shine' is reflected light. I've not had either experience.

A Bigfooter from Oregon, Big Geoff, was relegated, because there were no camp spaces available, to set up his tent at California Camp which was a few hundred yards up the road from Rock Camp. On his way back to his campsite he could hear what sounded like footfalls in the woods beside him. When he stopped, the steps from beside him made one more step. Thinking that he might be abducted by whatever was beside him, he got on his walkie-talkie and confessed his feelings - kind of reciting his last will and testament. He made it through the night with spurts of sleep, but heard a loud thump a few yards from him. In the morning, the sound he heard was explained by a 2-man rock (a rock that would take two men to lift) that had been on one side of the road, resting on the opposite side of the road – 15 feet away! It appeared to have been thrown.

This camping experience increased my appetite for further adventures in the search for Bigfoot

~ 8 ~

BF Trip 3

The Olympic Project

July-2012

This particular outing turned out to be very interesting in that Eryn and I seemed to be the only "guests" to a camp habituated by experienced and notables in the Bigfoot realm. As my daughter explained it, "This is like being invited backstage to a member's only Bigfoot event." Because of my lack of knowledge of the Who's Who in Bigfooting, I felt like I was the character Lenny in Steinbeck's *Of Mice and Men*, who says, "Tell me again --- (in my case) who are these people?" I probably should mention that I had never seen the TV show *Finding Bigfoot* nor had I ever read articles or books about Bigfoot. You might say I was out of the BF loop.

Unlike my previous outings, the Olympic Project is not located in the Cascade Mountain Range, but rather in the vicinity of the Hoh Rain Forest, Sol Duc Hot Springs and Crescent Lake. The acreage in the Olympic National Forest, is owned and managed by Derek Randles, cofounder/Investigations. He is not associated with BFRO or WABFR, so doesn't attract BF looky-loos, but mostly caters to experienced Bigfoot aficionados. Derek had a BF encounter in 1985 while in the Olympic National Park.

A good-sized barnlike building acted as a headquarters/showroom/ display area, with a shower and toilet facility. Camping spots were located in a woodsy area at the base of a mountainous range. There were hiking trailheads located just behind and beside the tent area. A bunkhouse was available to honored, elderly or handicapped guests. A large fire pit was situated near the barn and bunkhouse.

On the website www.olympicproject.com their mission statement says: *Association of dedicated researchers, biologists and teachers committed to documenting the existence of Sasquatch.* Their mantra: *Research with a purpose.*

Of the assembled group, we'd only previously camped with two searchers, Tyler (of *Finding Bigfoot*) and Nate. That night *Bob Gimlin*, the Godfather of Bigfooters, came into our midst. Many of the group in camp were an interesting combination of backgrounds. There were wildlife and field biologists, zoologists, audio/video/data analysts, field researchers, TV personalities and even people in the vicinity who'd had contact with Bigfoot --- and Eryn and me. Also, I learned a person in our midst had been struck by lightning. However, I avoided shaking hands with him for fear of being electrocuted even if he didn't glow in the dark.

Sitting around the campfire, I rubbed shoulders with:

Bobo (James Fay) of *Finding Bigfoot* who had come with his dog Monkey.

Dr. **John Bindernagel** (*The Discovery of the Sasquatch; North America's Great Ape: the Sasquatch),* and his wife, Joan. [Dr. Bindernagel passed away in 2018]

Cliff Barackman Co-host of *Finding Bigfoot* and maker and displayer of a collection of foot casts from many geographical areas.

Tyler Bounds - BFRO investigator and outdoor tech for *Finding Bigfoot.*

Paul Graves – Longtime Sasquatch researcher, musician/composer of Bigfoot songs. He performed a BF song dedicated to and mentioning Bob Gimlin. Paul demonstrated his musical skills by accompanying our singing with his guitar.

Dave Ellis – Listed as an audio/visual analyst – is also a Master Caster of BF prints

John Andrews – Since 1958 has done field research and investigations of 100s of sightings. He is an extreme hiker, according to those who try to keep up with him.

Bob Gimlin – Famous for what's known as *The Patterson-Gimlin Bigfoot Film* (1967) which documents a Bigfoot sighting of a female BF. Born in 1931, Bob continues to make appearances at various Bigfoot gatherings.

Other Bigfooters I would meet in the future and who are on the Olympic Project roles, but weren't at this gathering:

Cindy Caddell – Professional photographer that is also a field researcher/photo analyst.

Barb Olvera –is a field researcher with a degree in Biology.

There were Bigfooters from other states at this gathering who contributed to our expansion of knowledge of things Bigfoot/Sasquatch. A zoologist researcher from California and I "took" to one another in a father-daughter sort of way, with her calling me Dad.

During the day we congregated at the building to look at displays of pictures, foot casts, books, etc., plus we had a chance to meet and talk to notables and common folks about anything related to our gathering. Because of extensive trails around and up the foothills, we were encouraged to take a hike. Some brave souls, including Eryn and two other girls, slept on a portion of a trail one night.

(L) Dr. John Bindernagle, the author, Cliff Barackman, Robert, Kief

As we were saying goodbye to various campers, I came upon Bobo and told him I was glad that I had met him, and confessed I'd never watched *Finding Bigfoot*. His reply was, "No big deal – neither have I."

On our way back home we stopped at a store that had Bigfoot stuff, and had a restaurant featuring a Bigfoot Burger. It was HUGE! And took me about 45 minutes with Eryn's help to consume it. I know my stomach will always remember it as it tried to digest it in the three-hour trip. It reminded me of an old Alka Seltzer TV ad, where a man, with a look of misery, says, "I can't believe I ate the WHOLE thing!"

Dr. John Bindernagle & the author

~ 9 ~

BFRO Mount Adams

Late July – 2012

After a two week rest and recovery from our Olympic Project Expedition, we headed east and into the Cascade Mountains, near Mount Adams. The expression, 'Getting there is half of the fun' applied to the route we traveled. The roads had highway numbers, like 23 and 88, but some of the road surfaces were in sad condition due to weather damage. Speed limit signs were unrealistic and sparse. The roadway had signs posted saying Pavement Ends (like for 10 miles), and suddenly a section of pavement appeared for a few miles, then back to dirt. There was a sign advising drivers Roadwork Ahead, with the 'Ahead' road crew 20 miles from the sign. The scenery was very impressive and appeared to be prime habitat for the elusive Bigfoot.

We eventually made our way to the BFRO campsite where a fairly large group Bigfooters were setting up camp. We staked out a site near a game trail and alongside other tents, unloaded our gear and wandered around meeting our fellow Bigfoot trekkers. Nadia, from California, Tyler and Nate from our Olympic Project campout were with us again, plus Ric, Peter, Col. Kevin, Scott, Rayn, Barb, Beth, John R., et al. from our previous BFRO and WABFR Expeditions were also in the camp. Newbies who made impressions were David Bakara from Florida, Kat, Mike B★ (see his cougar encounter report at the end), Ghee, and

Torrie. I mention these names because they would appear in other BF get-togethers.

As in other Bigfoot gatherings, various groups were formed for night walks. It's thought by experienced Bigfooters that BF comes out of the woods to checkout bunches of people who walk down mountain or forest roads with red head lamps, periodically stopping in order to let out a howl and listen for a response. Personally, I get a bit nervous or embarrassed when a male-caller lets out a call that sounds like a girl with a sore throat. But the first time I heard a response from a distance, I could see it was like a calling card to let any distant Squatches know we are in their domain.

My group of about 12 night walkers headed out of camp at a pretty good clip, which puts me at the rear. Whoever's bringing up the rear is known as "cougar-bait," because cougars attack their prey from the rear. I was joined by Torrie. We were about a half-mile out, when she asked me if I was being struck by pebbles or pine cones, because she was. Suddenly, she grabbed my hand and said she was getting sick and felt like something was somehow attacking her. I told our group leader that we needed to stop in order to let her rest. When she explained the feeling she had, the group encircled her and sat beside the road. As we sat, it became apparent a lightning storm was approaching in the distance. We couldn't hear the sound of accompanying thunder even as the flashes got closer – THEN, all hell broke loose with lightning, thunder, wind and torrential rain! Our orderly night walk devolved into a helter-skelter run back to camp. I've been in hurricanes, typhoons and blizzards, but this mountain storm beats them all. Kids and women were screaming as we were guided by lightning light to the safety (?) of our water and lightning-proof (ha-ha) tents. The rain was so intense that it was nearly impossible to see where we were going. When reaching our tent, I cursed myself for not fastening the fly. Inside the tent was a virtual wading pool. As the storm passed by, I bailed what I could with a cooking pan, then cut a couple of slots for a drain at the lower end of the tent. When Eryn returned from her walk – er – run, she opted to take her sleeping bag and spend the night in someone's tent that had thought to close their fly. I wished that somebody had said to me, "Hey, your fly's open!" One couple and their young son had had their tent blown over and all of their bedding, clothes and equipment was soaked. They spent the night in their vehicle, and ended up leaving at daylight. Fortunately, I had the opportunity to converse with the guy during the previous day and asked him if he had any Bigfoot experiences. He related an experience in a Southern State when he and a couple of college friends camped during a Spring Break. About dusk he took a roll of toilet paper and headed out of their site in order to do his "business." While on his purposeful trek he suddenly came upon a Bigfoot. As soon as they saw each other both turned around and ran back to where they came from. Thinking his buddies wouldn't believe him, no mention was made of it until they were on the way home when the incident was relayed. One of the campers said he also had a similar experience, but didn't bring it up because he thought the others wouldn't believe *him*. The third guy thought the two who told their tales were "full of it" and were just trying to freak him out.

The morning after the storm I woke up about 4:00 AM to the sound of two individuals (judging from two different voice pitches) having a conversation in an unfamiliar language. I thought to myself the sound was like animals talking to each other. When I reported this to the BFRO organizers, they told me I'd heard Bigfoot talking. Hmmm...

When we all got together to talk about our experiences of the previous night, there were three tents sitting near our gathering, to dry out, when a large gust of wind scooped up all three tents, turned them over and set them right-side-up a few yards away.

During the day, we explored our environs in hopes of finding signs of BF habitation. I discovered what appeared to be elk bones, located just off a game trail, while campers Ghee and Mike went way out and upland for some extreme exploring.

That night I got behind the steering wheel of a vehicle labeled "R-2 D-2" (of *Star Wars*) because of device mounted on its roof looking like a TV dish. In actuality, this roof hardware is a Thermal Eye 500 XP (or something similar) that can locate anything that radiates heat. The dish is able to be rotated 360 degrees by a joystick operator in the vehicle. In this case the person working the joystick was a 12-year-old video-game-pro named Hunter. A small screen receives the image for the operator to view. As a driver, I drove very slowly on the logging roads in the vicinity of our camp while Hunter did his stuff. Occasionally, I'd be told to stop or back up if something appeared to be suspicious. In over a two-hour period we spotted several deer or elk, but nary a Bigfoot.

All in all, this trip turned out to be a Bigfoot blast.

★ Cougar Encounter

"The encounter happened on a September, 1996 morning at daybreak. I was on a game trail near Wilcox farms close to Heart Lake not far from the town of Roy, Washington. I was sitting in some large ferns next to a mature Fir tree. As the sun began to rise with a low fog in the valley below me and a chill in the air I prepared myself and my bow for a deer to wander up the trail as I have taken several from that very spot over the years. I began to hear the sounds of squirrels cutting fir cones and dropping them in preparation for winter. I looked in the direction of the sounds to confirm the source. The air was still and as the sun finally rose above the trees and the rays filtered through the forest. As I sat there taking in the view, two deer in the flats below me started heading up the hill my way after a night of filling their bellies under a full moon. I was focused on them waiting for my chance to harvest one and it would still be a 30 minutes or longer as they grazed their way to me, I was in no hurry. I had a small bird, a wren, hanging out near me to entertain me and keep me company. Suddenly I heard a noise behind me I looked but saw nothing. I began to turn my head back toward the approaching deer and at that moment *I was hit from behind* knocking me down on all fours. I felt the pain of claws sinking into my back on the left side low just under my day pack. At first I thought it was a bear however as it went over the top of me and the claws came out of my back catching my pack then the back of my head tearing the top of my ear away from my head then plunging into my right temple I saw *it was a Cougar.* It had jumped on me in a way that caused it to be crossed up. Its right claws caught my left side as its left arm went over my right shoulder then as we went forward her left hip hit the Fir tree with enough forced it caused her to bounce off of it releasing my head. It was then as I looked at my bow and noticed the arrow was no longer in the rest but still in the saddle. I looked up at the Cougar and she got up and got her feet under her, then showed her teeth and I was looking her in the eye at about eight feet from me. Its eyes dilated, then it pounced toward me. I sat up and pulled my bow string back slightly then released the arrow. It looked as if it was going to miss its target but somehow struck her in the right shoulder bending the arrow shaft causing the arrow to catch a rib then it passed through its lungs killing it.

I then ran to my vehicle about two miles away and looked at my injuries in my reflection on the glass of my passenger door. The bleeding had stopped. I drove to town and got a tag then went back and threw it over my shoulders and carried it out. I took it home and then went to the hospital where I got 12 stitches inside my back and 16 on the outside. They taped my ear as it wasn't bad enough to need stitching and they put a bandage on my temple. I got some shots and some pills. It took over a year for my temple to heal. I was getting bone chips coming to the surface in the area of my temple for two plus years.

The cat turned out to be a 7ft 6 inch female which is number nine in the State Record Books.

Michael Beers "

This tale gave impetus to the meaning of being called "cougar bait." I thought about wearing a Halloween mask on the back of my head on future walks.

Mt. Adams' Bigfoot Bunch

Just the two of us with the mountain behind us

~ 10 ~

Near Chinook Pass - 8/16-19/2012

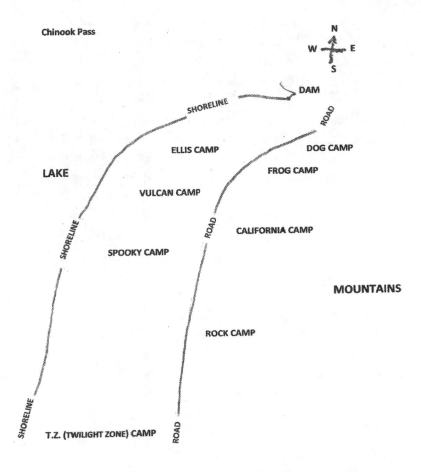

Campsite locations near Chinook Pass

Eryn & I (Dad/Don) arrived at California Camp around 1:30 PM on Thursday. Kevin's & Kirk's tents were set up at Rock Camp. Ted, a seasoned Bigfooter, pulled in and got positioned with his camper. He and trusty companion, Beta (his dog), set "bait" (banana, dog biscuit, McDonald French fries) on a stump. These items had previously attracted something to peel and eat three bananas. This time Ted wanted to set up a camera (Trail-cam) to find out what was eating the bananas. The first night without a camera the banana wasn't touched --- but something took the dog biscuit. 2nd night – banana and fries were untouched, but once again the dog biscuit got removed. Ted replaced the untouched banana with a new one. The old banana, a yam (?) and a plum were taken to a stump in Main Base Camp across the road. Long story short – nothing got taken at MBC, but something continued taking the dog biscuit at California Camp. Robber jays? The jays and a loud raven (wing flapping & caws) finally decided to take all the fries. Yet, the banana survived. Nothing showed up on the trail-cam to explain the missing dog biscuits – dogs?

Kevin wanted to set up a camp at distant Lily Lake, so set out with me, Kat, and James plus a kayak, & tent to stake out a claim on the island. Later, another kayak, supplies and cameras and/or recorders were transported to the island where they spent the night – no activity.

Saturday, when I was walking the road from Rock Camp to California Camp, I became aware of being tracked from the woods alongside the road. Although I wasn't able to see anything, I could hear something almost the entire length of the walk.

Lee, Anita and I spent time looking for signs of BF in the woods alongside the road and behind large trees & stumps where they might hide – and spotted some suspect prints. I noticed across game trails where there were rotting downfalls, there were depressions like something stepped on them, probably not deer or elk because they would step over them, as indicated by their tracks. Was BF using them like stepping stones?

Darrel, an excellent and experienced tracker, found several prints behind Rock Camp, from which he and Ghee got a good cast. Darrel, on a previous trek, slept in/on the bed of his pickup truck, and when he woke in the night met with the sight of a BF looking at him from the tailgate!

It seems like almost every time I go on a BF campout I come home all banged up. I got a big hematoma at Morton, a skinned knee and elbow at Trout Lake (Big Tire), and a banged up and bloody arm & leg this trip. As Kevin said, "Nobody has gotten injured in our outings - - - - - except Don." (Scott threatened to wrap me in bubble-wrap in future outings.) I was out in the woods across from CA Camp with Kevin, looking for walking sticks with growth bulges at one end. I managed to get three of them and was returning to camp and stepped over a fairly high downfall and managed to crash against a tree with little stubbles of branches. When I returned to camp with my bloody prizes, my campmates dug into their first aid kits – Laura took charge like a nurse by cleaning and sterilizing my wounds & covering the mess while Kevin wrapped it, and Ted supplied Gorilla Tape to hold it all together. It didn't look particularly pretty, but it did the job and I didn't need a transfusion. My wife asked me when I got home, "Why do they let you come on these trips, anyway?"

(left) Ted, Col. Kevin, Eryn, Bob Gimlin, Darrel and Don

When Ted's in camp, he makes some wicked jambalaya, chili, and farmer breakfasts. One evening Su brought a watermelon which Ted sliced with his machete. He also let Laura cook little cakes steamed in hollowed-out oranges wrapped in foil on his camp stove. Nice! After dinner everyone told their experiences with Bob Gimlin, who amazes us with his life stories. Of course, Kevin comes up with some entertaining & interesting tales – er – experiences.

It's kind of strange to sit a camp fire ring with no fire in it, but it doesn't dampen BF experiences being told in the glow of a Coleman lantern or even no light. Calls of various types come from various outposts throughout the night, but the "Theme from the *Star Trek* series" performed by the incomparable Laura Roeder got the most amazing and numerous reactions I've ever heard. Coyotes went wild! A Spokane couple were at our camp one night, and Donnel saw the Glow stick on Eryn's and my tent get moved around and periodically blocked. When I lay in the tent, I could hear activity around the tent and in particular near the stick.

Laura and Mike had visual sightings in the same vicinity at different times. Eryn was with Laura when she saw BF, but Eryn was looking in the wrong direction. Darn! These run-across-the –road experiences recall the spate of experiences with *streakers* back in the 80s.

It was great seeing those I know, and meeting others for the first time. I enjoy camping with all of the Bigfooters and love the enthusiasm of like-minded folks.

Near Chinook Pass #3 Report - Laura Roeder

8/16/12: Laura gave her permission to print *her version* of events for this expedition.

Arrived approx. 5:30pm. Made camp at California. Approx. 9:00pm, occupied Spooky Camp (halfway to end of road) with Eryn and Kathleen. Dark camp as there was a burn ban. Eryn and I planned to individually occupy Kevin's tents, right next to each other and Kathleen planned to sleep in her vehicle.

Heard some twig snaps while there were just three of us, then Guy and James hiked from Rock Camp down to our location and talked for a while. During that time we heard more movement around us and discovered we could hear Brock's camp extremely well from this location. They did several calls and we had to verify if it was them over the radio, as they had not announced prior. They agreed to announce from that point on.

After Guy and James left, we went to bed, but I didn't hear anything the rest of the night. The batteries in my Edirol had gone dead, so I couldn't record, but Kathleen did. Woke the next morning, not sure the others got anything on the recorder during the night.

8/17: Returned to California camp, changed and got breakfast at the marina with several others. Went back to California and chatted for a while. Went to Lilly Lake with Kevin to scout and when we returned, went to the launch on the lake with Eryn for the afternoon and kayaked. Returned, had dinner with the group.

Eryn and I decided to stay at California for the night. Eryn went to Spooky camp to retrieve Kevin's tents while I was making dessert with Kirk and Ted. After dinner, many vehicles started arriving in the area, as the campgrounds had reached capacity. As darkness fell, we heard some movement beyond the latrine. It seemed very quiet, and moving fairly consistently, not a plodding of hooves, but rather like very soft steps and an occasional twig snap. Dale said he'd noticed the glow stick on Eryn and Don's tent was obscured from time to time. Some movement was also heard near the road as well. Ted's dog Beta alerted several times from the interior of the camper. I saw green eye shine behind Eryn's Jeep once and Dale indicated that he had seen some as well.

As the evening progressed, Kirk radioed that he was going to walk to California camp from Vulcan, aka Spooky, camp (they abut each other). Since we thought it was funny that "Kirk" was coming from the "Vulcan" camp, I decided to sing the female vocal from the old Star Trek series for fun. Surprisingly, when I ended, many coyotes started howling in response for about 5 minutes. Everyone laughed and there was radio chatter about the source of the vocal. Kirk then radioed that a vehicle had pulled into Vulcan camp and then exited and instead pulled into Spooky camp, just beyond the spot where we had been the night before. It was a small group with two vehicles. A very loud sound emanated from Spooky several times in response to calls and whistles that our group was doing that sounded like a recording of a Sasquatch that had a great amount of background noise in it. Kirk turned around and proceeded to Spooky to see if they were Squatchers. He radioed after some minutes that they were, but were not "friendly" and they did not wish Kirk and his companions to remain in their camp. Su walked out to meet Kirk at Vulcan camp a short while after arriving around midnight.

Movement continued to a certain extent near California, but any calls that were done by our camps were met with an extremely loud audio blast from the group at Spooky, which seemed to potentially quell the movement. Went to sleep in Eryn's tent and Don went to sleep in mine to try the cot out.

Not sure of the hour, but I heard Su come back to camp from either Vulcan or Rock, and exited in her car. Approximately 5 minutes after she left, I heard a single, deep huff-like sound from the direction of the latrine. Approximately 15 minutes after that, I heard what sounded like a large tree break or large object crushing another one from across the road, some yards into the timber. I called to Eryn, (we had an agreement that it was OK to wake the other if we heard something during the night), but she didn't wake at first, but then woke on my second call. She hadn't heard it at all. We both went to sleep and I didn't hear anything during the night.

8/18: Breakfast at camp. Visited with others and heard accounts of the previous night. Went to Rock camp to see the cast that Guy and James had gotten near Rock. Talked with others for a while, hiked up to the location where the cast had been taken, then Eryn and I went to the second bridge and walked up the creek for a bit. Eryn crossed to see if there were prints. Nothing found, we proceeded to Twilight Zone and had lunch. Saw Bob Gimlin go by as we were exiting the trail and said hi as he made his way to the turn around and then started back for California camp around 1:00pm. After Eryn and I crossed the 2nd bridge, we had gone some miles and were approaching a little bend in the road. Eryn was looking off to the right as the passenger and I was driving.

Suddenly, ahead and on the right side of the road, I saw a dark brown, almost black humanoid figure come from behind some young, lighter green evergreens with what appeared to be a kind of lurching movement with its left shoulder. It ran across the road at an amazing speed and I yelled out loud from the surprise. The left side of the road was partially obscured from view due to the bend so I only saw it for about a second, but it did not look like a person (it was all one color), deer, elk, bear or cat at all. Eryn asked if I had just seen one, and I said yes. She then commented that this was approximately the same place where Mike had seen one the previous day.

I stopped the Jeep and we got out to look for any sign. Neither of us could find any after searching for a while. We returned to camp. We told the group there, but Mike was not present to verify the size or color that he had seen the day before. (He did contact me via Facebook this afternoon and he verified that his sighting was of the same color, and approximately the same height- there was some variance, as he said it was in the ditch portion when he saw it).

Broke camp and spent the last few hours at California talking with several others and said farewells. Departed for home at 4:00pm.

Walking to the lake

~ II ~

Near Chinook Pass - Report 9/20-23/2012

I've been on six Bigfoot campouts (May to September) this year, but this search was the most memorable.

When Eryn and I drove over Chinook Pass, we were greeted by the unpleasant sight of columns of smoke rising from several places where lightning had started spot fires. Our first trip to this area was in May when snow was still in the woods. This time it was extremely dry and a cloud of dust followed us down the road on our way to our campsite.

A number of Bigfooters from previous encampments were setting up camps along the camp road leading up to *Rock Camp* (main site). Upon our arrival at Rock Camp we were greeted by, Ted & Beta, and "master caster" Dave Ellis. Dave wanted to set up his large Cabela© tent at Frog Pond, aka Dog Camp (Later, Robert, Kristine with their windowless camper/toy hauler, and Paull Graves set up at that location, too) so Eryn and I went with Dave to give him a hand. It was like trying to figure out a jigsaw puzzle, but a half hour later - mission accomplished!

The nearby lake was being lowered in order to prepare for the runoff of the coming season which exposed much more shoreline. Besides a quantity of lost fishing gear, there were a fair number of barefoot impressions leading from the forest to the lake's edge. They were unlikely to be barefoot campers because of their semi-remote location, but they were of a smaller than those of a large creature. It was surmised that they were juvenile and female Squatch prints, and perhaps the larger BF stayed in the woods as "watchers" or guards. Anyway, there were lots of prints, which gave us a chance of making casts under the guidance of Dave Ellis, aka "Master-Caster." In appreciation of helping setting up his tent, the "master" took us to the lake to hunt and cast footprints in the mud. Col. Kevin, Barbara, Tracy, and Kat joined us after a while. Eryn and Kat got some good ones, and I had my first experience of seeing a trail of clear prints.

A night later, Bob Gimlin, joined us in Rock Camp. Most of the Rock Campers went thither and yon in the dark to see if they could scare up some action. Everybody but Nate, Bob, Ted and I were left in camp. Bob said, "I'm getting a bit stiff just sitting here, is anybody up for a walk?" Geez, a night walk with Bob Gimlin strikes me as an Elvis fan getting asked if they'd like to hang out with the "King." Needless to say, we tripped all over ourselves to get going. Our little group had ages from the 20s (Nate), 60s (Ted), 70s (me), 80s (Bob). Nate had a glow-in-the-dark soccer ball that he kicked in front of us as we walked along. We figured if the ball got picked up and rolled back, we might have made contact with our "hidden friends." We walked the ½-mile to Dog Camp where we visited with their campers. Since we couldn't sit around the usual campfire, a battery powered lamp with a red cap set over it (for ambience) was placed in a flameless fire pit.

It was suggested that somebody should give a Bigfoot howl to see if we might get a response, so Paul Graves volunteered. About a minute after disappearing into the woods in the direction of the Pond, we heard a melodious howl. A second or so later two separate responses were heard. Encouraged by this, he let out another call. The response was closer and sounded like an elk rather than a Bigfoot. Bob said something like, "You might want to stop the calls because you're bringing in elk. This is their rutting season and the calls might be misinterpreted." It continued to get closer and closer, and by the time Paul made it back, up to our circle, we could practically hear its breathing.

Bob decided he'd sat long enough, so suggested we might walk to the dam (a good distance from where we were) to which Ted responded,

"Are you s----ing me?" Instead, we directed our steps to Old Main Base Camp, aka Ellis Camp, (between Dog Camp and Rock Camp) because we had seen a vehicle drive to that location. Our suspicions were confirmed and we were greeted by Dale, Donnel, Annie (Dale's mom) and their 11-year-old grandson.

On our trek back to Rock Camp Bob continued to amaze us with his undiminished agility and told us of his daily walking regimen of walking six to seven miles a day. His doctor told him to knock off his 13-mile daily jog, after his bypass surgery, and slow down. He agreed to cut down the distance, but told the doctor, "Doc, my shoes are broken in to move fast and I can't seem to slow them down."

Back at Rock Camp all the night-walkers gathered to relate any experiences, mainly relating to the rutting-elk activity, and some red eye-glow sighting. Dale, from Spokane, reported he'd seen red glow from a "one-eyed" BF on previous trips.

The "Night Walkers" Ted, Bob Gimlin. The Author, Nate

Michelle and friend, Jeremy-the-cook, set up in, what they called, Log Camp, but joined us a Rock camp at meal time. Michelle works at Cabela's and showed up with some "slick" camping gear and accessories like a compact camping stove that's fueled with little sticks and has a fan that keeps the fire going as long as it's fed. It also somehow charges the fan-batteries as well as phone batteries. It's like a self-perpetuating machine that doesn't stop working as long as you feed it sticks.

As usual, Mike and Ghee fearlessly challenge the unknown with their trekking into the hinterlands at unseemly nighttime and early morning hours. Doug, a Bigfoot magnet, was only with us a short time, but joined forces with the two adventurers.

First-timer, Lee, came with Scott and spoke of his (seasonal) "Screaming–Man-of-Ashford" experiences. Very interesting.

Laura, Eryn and Su, as usual, were up to camping out at night wherever suspected activity might take place. Su camps in her VW Bug very comfortably – thank you. I'll have to say these ladies are just about the most enthusiastic hunters of Bigfoot forest people you'll ever run into.

We seemed to have a lot of nighttime activity with Doug seeing obstruction of glow sticks, and Big Geoff having a Class-A (actual) sighting. Some eye shine, knocks and howls (Class-B) were experienced by others, including Nate and I who both heard what sounded like monkey chatter early one morning.

With all our BF experiences discussed, we *Rock Campers* hit the sack. Big Geoff left us in order to return to *California Camp*. On his trip back he could hear something walking beside him. If he stopped, the "walker" in the woods beside him would stop, etc. Back at his campsite he thought he might relieve his nerves by playing some classical music on his guitar. While he played he could hear humming behind him. (Do elk hum?) Hmmm…

The next day Col. Kevin took some of us to various natural and Squatch sites like Rattlesnake Ridge, Columnar Rock formations, Devil's

Canyon and Bear Cave. It was necessary to climb up steep terrain to explore the cave. Not qualifying as a limber or steep-terrain climber, I explored the area near the road where a terrible smell emanated. I'd heard that sometimes BF smells very rank, so cautiously sought out the source. It was the haunch of a deer. Maybe it was Bigfoot lunch. No carcass was anywhere to be seen – just a haunch.

Upon our return from our side trip, there were some new campers who'd arrived. Most notable was a large white Humvee-type vehicle driven by a Canadian father/son team. They called their vehicle a "Squatch-Mobile." It had been bought as surplus from a Canadian agency which intended to use it for emergency situations, like …?

Other Bigfooters came throughout the day and into the night. Mel Skahan, a timber-cruiser and forest manager for the 700,000 acre Yakima Indian Reservation, visited briefly, but long enough to make an impression on me concerning the existence of Bigfoot in Native American lore over the centuries and their present coexistence. (Later on at another BF trek I was privileged to visit with him for several hours)

At the end of this Bigfoot Expedition, while we cleaned up our camps and made ready to return to our normal homes, the smoke from the forest fires moved into our area. I don't know if it was the smoke or the fact that this was our final BF hunt of the season for most of us, but I sensed some teary-eyed farewells.

~ 12 ~

BFRO Expedition on 6/12-16/13

Eryn's Expedition

Eryn, who's been an organizer for events, starting with horse shows, contests, etc. at the age of eight, applied to BFRO Headquarters in order to do an Expedition in the Cascade Mountains near Morton. Col. Kevin mentored and assisted her in this complex event with BFRO providing publicity. Newcomers had to be vetted because of applications coming in from several states, and even Sweden. The TV show *Finding Bigfoot* had stimulated nationwide interest in this outdoor activity, causing many more applications to go Bigfooting than could be accommodated.

Eryn & I arrived in the area around noon to set up and mark the way to Main Base Camp after briefly talking with Kirk who had come in and set up a satellite camp a day before. As we were talking, Tom from Colorado drove up and offered to help us with rock cairns which were used to identify the logging road to take into the BF camping area.

We set up camping tents and one for a toilet facility, digging a very deep hole, which filled up a day short of striking camp. The facility was moved and served us well. Tents and trailers began coming in on Friday and into Saturday, plus several Bigfooters chose to camp at outposts outside of MBC within walkie-talkie range.

Col. Kevin set up a large tarp (30'X40') on a frame, and had two gas-powered fire pits, a large gas stove, and some tables used to display Sasquatch books (supplied by Laura), foot casts and maps. The tarp covering was especially appreciated Thursday and Friday showers.

Gathering in the tent

Newbies came from Sweden, Georgia, Colorado, New Mexico, Wisconsin, Oregon and various parts of Washington. All seemed rarin' to go. It was great seeing old-timers from last season, too. It was a great mix of serious Sasquatch researchers. We also had many laughs and interesting observations. The two men from Georgia were Wounded Warriors who were so impressed with the whole experience that they presented Eryn a special Wounded Warrior coin. A writer/photographer for *National Geographic* joined our bunch for a couple of days in order to add to her material she was doing for a segment called "What People do at Night." Besides night scenes in cities, night walks in search for Bigfoot appealed to her journalistic-sense. Somehow I was brought in front of her camera's lens, and was immortalized and even displayed in a photo collection in Colorado where one of my college friends saw it and recognized me (even after more than 50 years).

Workshops were given on first aid in the woods (as well as plants to avoid) by RN John; casting by veteran Bigfooter, Scott; using R-2, D-2 (heat sensing gizmo used in the cool of the night); driving and walking destinations; recognizing signs of Big Foot, etc.

Several Squatch sounds were heard and recorded, plus some eye shine (reflected from ambient light sources [the moon] and possible prints. But the R-2 D-2 treks up and down the mountain sides only revealed deer and critters the size of rabbits.

I went on night walk with Tyler, Nate, Maryellen and Renae. The two ladies were the ER the nurses who picked me up after I bit the dust (rocks) on my first night walk in 2012, so under directions from my daughter they walked on either side of me in case of another accident.

**Maryellen, the author and Renae
setting out for a night walk**

Tyler is an extreme night-walker who sets a frenetic pace, stopping only occasionally to let out a whoop, which allows his followers to catch up. We let out with some whoops, but couldn't hear the responses that were heard at MBC. We did hear clacks sent out by John R on a hilltop a couple of miles away. We also could hear Scott from an equal or further distance. We didn't hear suspicious noises until we got about a quarter of a mile from MBC, when an owl let us know we were in its territory.

Nate, another energetic night-walker, took a group of five newbies to a swampy area where they all saw at a distance of about 75 feet, a single bright LED-type light floating among nearby trees and above thick nettles. As they watched, the light weaved in between trees, lighting them up as it put on a one minute light show. Glow worm? Fire fly? Radiated dragon fly? Hmmm…

All in all, this Expedition was well-run and successful.

~ 13 ~

Monkey Rock

2013

**Don, Phoenix and Eryn ready to roll
in the Jeep to Monkey Rock**

All of the Bigfoot campouts up to this time were in established BF campsites over the years of reported BF sightings. It was decided to explore a possible new campsite in an area where hunters and campers reported suspected BF activity alongside an abandoned highway near Ashford. Because this was a new and relatively unexplored area for Bigfooters, a trial run for an expedition was set up in an upland forest area near a pond and a large boulder resembling the head of a monkey.

It's interesting to travel on an abandoned paved highway that once (and even now) has had center stripes and even a fog line painted on it. Over the years, foliage crept over what's remaining of the road's surface. Potholes and missing segments of the highway have made what was once a pleasant scenic drive into a highway from hell.

A fairly level space for setting up about six or seven tents was decided on for a base camp and became tent town for our small group of Bigfooters. Peter, an intrepid BF aficionado, became our next-door neighbor and set up a shelter for a shared mess (kitchen) tent. A toilet area proved to be challenging because of very difficult rocky ground. One of the campers had the foresight to bring a toilet seat with legs which is used in hospitals, and it was set above a plastic tall kitchen bag-lined five gallon bucket.

After establishing a base camp, we set out to explore our surroundings and looked for game trails, abandoned side roads and other camp spots. When I returned to camp a nap seemed to be in order. No sooner had I lay down, when Rayn showed up and decided to set up next to us. Her method of attracting Bigfoot was to play whale recordings at a maximum volume. Goodbye nap.

Other Bigfooters, including Eryn, had methods of letting our elusive woodland neighbors know we were in their neighborhood. Col. Kevin played a recording of a Tarzan yell; Eryn whistled or called; Laura sang or played panpipes; Nate played a banjo; I played *Oh, Suzanna* on my harmonica; others banged or tapped on drums, yelled, etc. It was similar to cooks on a cattle drive ringing a triangle, or a bugler in the military telling troops what to do. I guess that after a while, when you've been in the same area time after time, the sound becomes familiar to creatures, just as domesticated pets respond to your voice or whistle.

After dark we split into a couple groups to try to drum up some BF activity, but were unsuccessful, so headed back to camp to gather around the fire pit. Dave pulled his Barcalounger, aka front passenger seat of his vehicle, into the circle and offered me a sit-down. Sheer comfort, but difficult to get out of. So I extended my time in the seat.

Ric showed up on his motorcycle the next day to check out the site for an upcoming BFRO Expedition he planned to conduct in this area within the next few weeks. Eryn, Phoenix and I thought we would drive up the road to see where it led, but couldn't get her Jeep to start. All of the mechanically adept campers offered their assistance to get it up and running. After a couple of hours of trying everything known to man to assist us, nothing was successful. We were loaned a vehicle in order to find a fix to our problem. A tow truck was located that agreed to tow us over a hundred miles back home. We had to have Eryn's husband, a mechanic, come with his car to pick us up. The tow truck wouldn't drive up the mountain road to assist us, so Jax, Eryn's husband, had to coast the Jeep down 13 miles of the "Highway from Hell" without the aid of power bakes or steering. The tow truck hooked up the car once we got to a normal highway. Many hours later, and in the middle of the night, we got back home. The problem of the unstartable Jeep was a small part in the ignition system.

We hoped our next trip to Monkey Rock would be more enjoyable.

2nd Trip to Monkey Rock
Ric's Expedition

Two or three weeks after our untimely departure from our first trip, even with the repaired Jeep, we made the repeat journey in a rental. All the rest of our outings were done with car rentals.

A larger group made it to this Bigfoot camp location, so a few of us had to set up a short distance away beside the Highway from Hell and near the entrance of an overgrown logging road. Amazingly, some thoughtless folks had dumped furniture and other junk a little way up this road. Sad! We packed up much of the junk to haul out when we departed. I tried digging a hole for our group's potty tent in the rock-laden ground, semi-successfully, after what seemed like hours.

A couple of target shooters made a camp about 300 yards down the mountain, leaving a little after twilight without putting out their illegal campfire. So, Eryn, Laura and Susan took their chairs to this area and doused the still-burning fire, and where they conducted a "night-sit." While sitting in the dark they "witnessed a 'living' light that resembled a cross between a jellyfish and a 'white duck feather' as it smeared its way through the trees about three feet from them." Eryn stated that "It was as though it was thanking us for putting out the dangerous fire."

There were also other light-type phenomena happening within the forest by three different night- walking groups, like flashbulbs going off at many places and not fireflies (which we don't have in our part of the PNW.) I had a similar experience at the Olympic Project trip, but thought the flashes were from trail-cams. I later asked if this was so, and was informed the trail-cams don't use flashbulbs.

About 3:00AM some campers in the upper main camp heard what they said two Chinese women arguing in the woods by their tent.

There were no actual sightings, but interesting other-types of goings-on at this location of the Cascades.

We packed up ours and others' trash, chalking up one more Bigfoot outing.

~ 14 ~

Western Hood Canal

Mid July - 2013

Because we had made contact with Bigfooters in Western Washington and especially those closer to the Olympic Peninsula's Olympic Mountains, we knew some BF hunters who might be interested in exploring on our side of the Cascades. Word was sent out to any of the Western Bigfoot Bunch that might spend a weekend in the woods to meet us on a road marked with an orange life jacket hanging on a tree.

Eryn camped in this same area two times, once with an All-Girl Expedition. Not much BF activity occurred, but unknown sounds and lights had gotten their attention, and BF activity reports made it a good area to explore.

Dad & daughter in front of a stump by our campsite

We claimed a previously used camping spot with room for several tents and close to a small river. A dummy (unoccupied) tent was erected at the entrance of our selected camping area to discourage other potential campers. After pitching our tent, a toilet tent was set up and we spent time exploring the woods and river. Laura came around 4:00 pm and Dave G. arrived after work with his glow-in-the-dark basketball. Because of a burn ban we put a glow stick and basketball in the fire pit, pulled up our camp chairs; or in Dave's case, he took the passenger seat (which he called his hillbilly Barcalounger) out of his vehicle. We shared stories and food until it was time to hit the sack. The chance that we might have any Squatch activity was nil because a campsite about 75 yards away started setting off firecrackers from about 2:00 in the afternoon until 2:00 in the morning. Their laughter and loud conversation made their condition obviously alcohol-induced. When they ran out of firecrackers, out came their pistols.

I don't quite understand the minds of those who travel miles into the woods to dump trash, leave garbage, light and leave fires still burning after they leave, shoot guns, set off fireworks, and do other mayhem. But from the start, I discovered these irresponsible behaviors happened no matter where we went Bigfooting. The practices we learned from BF hunters were – Respect the forest, use common sense concerning camping and clean up and pack out your garbage. After all, it's not like we're on the moon and won't be bothered by other visitors to this location.

We went to a nearby town for coffee and lunch, then to a Ranger Station to report the fireworks. Back at camp, Dave accompanied me to confront the gun/fireworks campers. It was a bit intimidating to talk to rowdy campers with guns on a table, but I asked them if they would curtail their nighttime activities at a more reasonable time – to which they agreed.

We were able to sit around the fire pit with a fresh glow stick that night without the continuous banging sounds of exploding gun powder. Fifteen minutes after I went to bed, the others continued storytelling. As Eryn describes the following experience: "All was quiet and dark as the moon hadn't made its appearance from behind a mountain peak in the east. While the three sat around the glow stick, Eryn, who was facing southwest, saw an enormous white aperture open up and become a blinding white spotlight shining on her from high above the mountain she was facing. Dave, who was facing Eryn, saw it hit ONLY her face, but because it was so bright, jumped up and yelled, thinking the tent behind him had burst into flames. Laura sat to the left of Eryn was blinded in one eye because of the brightness. Don, who was on his cot in the tent and facing the direction of the spotlight, saw a flash though his closed eyelids and asked, 'What's going on?'" My wife, after hearing of this episode, said it sounded like the Biblical account of the bright light Saul experienced on the Road to Damascus. Hmmm…

Even though we had no BF activity, the experience was – shall I say - enlightening. I looked forward to another campout in this neck of the woods.

~ 15 ~

Oregon Cascades

2013

Oregon Bigfooters, Barb and Big Geoff, set up a BFRO Expedition in an area of the Oregon Cascades that had never been used by BF hunters, but had reports of close encounters with game hunters. The chosen area was above the 6,000' level and accessible on cringe-worthy dirt roads which meandered around stands of Douglas fir, hemlock and cedar trees. Campsites were spread out along a winding road that ended up in cleared area where we could gather in the evening.

One of the campers who set up by us was beyond middle age and from the Oregon-California area. He claimed to have had an encounter with two albino Squatches while hunting by himself, and joined this Expedition to hear other BF experiences and share his.

After everyone had set up, and toward evening, a small helicopter circled our area, and checked us out closely, then disappeared to a lower altitude and out of sight.

The next day our group attended or presented classes for newbies. Eryn gave a class on casting footprints while Phoenix and I brought her the materials she needed and cleaned up after class; John H, a traveling nurse, taught first aid for campers; Kurt H, a professional landscaper, conducted a plant identification class, plus others like Col.

Kevin, contributed their expertise on activities related to Bigfooting and camping in the woods.

Shortly after the classes, several vehicles drove up to our location as far as they could go before getting stuck. Logos painted on them identified Sheriff, Forest Service and State Patrol. Evidently we were "busted!" But for what? We were told to take them to our leader – that, being Big Geoff and backed up by Col. Kevin. The helicopter that had checked us out was the manager of a large timber company on whose land we were illegally camped. Evidentially, it was believed we were setting up for a rave (wild party). I asked a State Patrol officer sitting in his vehicle if he'd ever been so far off a highway before, and he laughed and said he was just following directions from higher-up the chain of command to check out reports of a possible wild bunch that might have to be apprehended. The sheriff, a woman, even brought a dog. When it was explained what we were doing, the situation was straightened out and BFRO Expedition T-shirts were given to the land manager, and we were granted permission to continue with our gathering. Somehow the organizers didn't know we were camped on private property. We were asked not to have open fires and pick up after ourselves.

A game hunter/mountain man, Chris C, from nearby Sweet Home, came to our camp to tell about his close encounter he and his son had while camped out near our location. They had used the area where they camped several times in the past with no idea of contact with Bigfoot or any other forest wildlife. After settling for the night, the noise of banging came from the area of their truck. Chris exited the tent and didn't see anything, but decided while he was out of the tent, to relieve himself. He got the feeling something or someone was watching him, so pointed his flashlight in the area, when his light lit up a large BF standing near him. He yelled for his son to come out of the tent. The Squatch didn't move, plus there was another one remaining immobile, (as Chris described it) "just watching." When flash-lighted, both BF turned their heads, but neither advanced nor retreated, so in a panic mode, the hunters made a beeline to their truck and left the area. The next day they tried to sort out their experience. The noise they heard coming from their truck was the sound of their large tool box being moved for the BF to search for doughnuts they had in the truck bed. Chris surmised that these must've been territorial Squatches that had seen these hunters before and knew them as game hunters who left gut piles behind after gutting their prey.

Before this BF encounter neither hunter had believed or even thought about such a creature; however, after their encounter Chris wanted to tell of this experience. To hear him tell his tale was quite believable. His son was so traumatized by the experience he didn't want to talk about it. The son's reaction might be classified as Post Bigfoot Trauma Syndrome (PBTS).

We didn't have any sights or sounds of Bigfoot on this outing, but we met and interacted with both old and new Bigfooters, and enjoyed the natural beauty of this area of the Cascades. During one night watch we observed what we thought was a bit strange – a supposed "star" moved in different directions. Hmmm…

~ 16 ~

BLUE MOUNTAINS

Venturing to Southeastern Washington in the summertime involves some traveling through extremely hot, at least for those of us from the Northwest, country. Rationalizing that the altitude of our Bigfoot camping area might be a tad cooler, Eryn, Phoenix and I looked forward to visiting a new area to explore in our BF quest.

Col. Kevin had visited the Blue Mountains many times on hunting trips where he had serendipitously sighted Bigfoot. He invited us to join him along with several other BF friends to what were called "Kevin's Campouts." All of us had been on several expeditions together, but not to this area.

Nate Helgeson's summer of 2014 BF Experiences in the "Blue's"

"I had spent five or six consecutive weekends in the same area. For hours on end I could knock back and forth with 3-5 different Sasquatch returning my knocks. And then they would always follow me back to my tent .9 miles south and continue to knock all hours of the night, each evening.

One weekend I invited Kevin, and Ted to come to my spot to experience what I had been experiencing for over a month. In the midst of the typical knocking with returns, I noticed two *very bright red eyes* glowing several feet off the ground as the creature slowly walked up the ridge we were on, and began pacing up and down the ridge. Its eyes were extremely bright red, and would flicker in and out as it walked behind the trees and other flora. I was the only one of us that noticed and watched, not believing my eyes. So I called Ted over to take a look with me, to confirm what I was seeing. He was completely floored at the sight. About 30 seconds later, the episode was over. I would say it was about 150 yards away. The moon was directly behind the being, and there was no other source of light at 5500' that could produce or reflect what Ted and I witnessed. The eyes were as bright red as the red lights on our headlamps.

I went back several times on my own in the following months, but the place was dead. "

Most of the "good" campsites were occupied by the time we arrived, but there were two barracks buildings in which some of our group chose to bed down. Nearby was a stable, corral and watering trough for horses. In the evenings we gathered at a covered picnic building containing a fireplace. One night we celebrated Scott's birthday and had birthday cupcakes provided by Laura. I gave him a present of a Sasquatch brand peperoni stick. We were visited by the daughter of Julie Scott, author of *Visits from the Forest People: An Eyewitness Report of Extended Encounters with Bigfoot.* Julie's encounters were on Harstine Island in Puget Sound. My dad, oldest brother and I used to campout on a beach there in the early 1950s. We weren't visited by any wildlife of any sort at night because our dad, who was the first to go to sleep, and could be labeled 'King of Loud Snorers', started snoring as soon as his eyes were shut.

Grandson & Grandpa by their home in "the Blues"

The first night Phoenix and I used our tent while Eryn sacked out on the porch of one of the barracks. About 2:00 AM I was awakened by the sound of what sounded like a herd of buffaloes – not that I've had that experience – stampeding next to our tent. I expected to be trampled at any second, but "lucked out." I managed to get back to sleep – or maybe passed out - soon after the danger had passed and our tent remained standing. In the morning I commented to Phoenix that the stampeding elephants was pretty exciting, wasn't it? His puzzled look was accompanied by, "What elephants?" I couldn't believe he hadn't heard the herd. When I looked outside it became evident that our tent was next to a game trail, probably used by elk, deer or mountain goats. It was confirmed by Dale and Janelle who were near us that they too had heard what I did and that I hadn't just dreamed it.

View of barracks from horse water

Col. Kevin drove Phoenix and me up a nearly impossible mountain 'road' (?) to a Forest Ranger Fire Lookout. The view from this lookout was absolutely spectacular! We were in Washington State, but could see both Oregon and Idaho from this site. And we could see the beginning of a forest fire that eventually developed into a major blaze many miles away.

On the second night our group divided into three, and because of the *super moon* we had excellent natural night vision.

Eryn describes the night's activities:

"Around 11pm on the full moon several of us took a night walk to meet with a carload of others. In the car were Scott, Susan, Laura and me. Scott. Eryn, Phoenix, Dale and Col. Kevin were walking. About ½ mile from camp on a main logging road, the walkers and car-riders met. At this point both groups heard what sounded like STOMPING noises from the wooded side of a clear-cut to their east. The bright moon was shining in their eyes and it was impossible to see further than 30 feet away. The sound was probably 50 feet away. It was a giant stomp, stomp, STOMP…..like a bipedal elephant following alongside the road. Whatever was making the stomping noise took about a dozen steps, then --- just ….. SILENCE.

Phoenix asked the guys, "Was that an elk!?"

He was hopeful, but we all laughed (nervously) and told him elk don't walk on two legs.

After waiting, whistling and listening for around 20 minutes the group continued on and crossed the road to a hilly area to the west side. The moon lit up a 50-acre level area that had been decimated by a fire a few years earlier.

The group headed up the hill at a quick pace, except for Laura who had hurt her knee on a previous BF outing. I (Eryn) stayed back with her while the rest of the group surged ahead. Because of the moonlight and lack of vegetation we were able to see the others. As Laura and I crested a hill, from a distance of 200 feet from a very small grove of trees we heard the sound of tremendous stomping ..... The two-legged elephant had returned ..... But this time it sounded like it was charging AT US!

We still **couldn't see** ANYTHING but a few trees which were lit up by the moon and silhouetted by the sky behind. There was no underbrush for anything to hide in, let alone anything that sounded big! It was getting louder and louder, and we could feel the ground shake. Laura and I turned to face the invisible charger and braced our arms to brace for an impact of some kind, but at about 90-feet away the sound changed direction to head west with no change of pace. Once again we saw NOTHING. The sound and vibration headed into a forest that was untouched by an old forest fire, and just stopped when it sounded like it hit the timberline. It must have traversed 350-feet in 20-seconds.

I yelled out to the group who were several acres away and they shouted back, "What in the heck was that?!" Phoenix was now understandably convinced that the sound was not an elk.

After spending another hour of looking around on the hill and at the edges of the timberline the group only heard several whistles and tree breaks from deeper inside the forest. There were no footprints or any signs that anything, including a bipedal pachyderm had traveled across the 50-acre expanse."

After our Blue Mountaintop expedition was over and we headed back to a cooler Puget Sound.

Scenery at the bottom of the Blue Mountains

We stopped at a Yakima McDonald's in order to get a cool drink. It was 110-degrees!

~ 17 ~

Final Trip on the Olympic Peninsula

July 2016

A few of our Olympic Peninsula Bigfoot Friends gathered at a camping area where BF had been sighted by practically everyone (but me) on previous excursions. Besides camping and hoped-for encounters, Eryn was scheduled to be interviewed via phone by Mel Skahan for a radio program emanating from the Yakima Reservation, concerning Sasquatch.

Upon our arrival, Scott and Susan Taylor, Ron Morehead and Keri Campbell had made camp at the edges of a cleared area where cars could park. The cleared area was cluttered with fireworks litter from the previous night (4th of July) and the people who set them off were camped a little ways off, consisting of three women and one man. They claimed to be locals. While Scott went to work picking up the litter, a Park Ranger came into our midst and asked for our Discovery Pass, required for vehicles in State Parks, which we had but the "locals" didn't. They had two vehicles and were cited for not having the required passes, plus they were told to pack up and clean up their camping spot. The man disappeared into town (?) while the women cleaned up their space, leaving one lady to wait for the man to return to pick up their camping gear. About 11:00PM he showed up, all "juiced-up" and mad as a trapped wildcat because of being "caught." For, what seemed like, the next three hours he loudly expressed his displeasure by using the "F" bomb several hundred times while packing out and throwing armloads of camp gear into his car.

As mentioned earlier, Ron Morehead (*Sierra Sounds, Voices in the Wilderness*) joined our group because he had recently moved into our area, and would accompany Eryn for the phone interview and promote his upcoming book, *Quantum Bigfoot: 40 years of searching the Bigfoot enigma*. Ron is one of the biggest names in the Bigfoot realm, traveling the world studying Bigfoot evidence. Plus - He is a worldwide speaker/lecturer, explorer, diver, adventurer, pilot and entertainer/musician. All this, yet in his presence, he's just a seemingly "normal" guy, like most of those of prominence in the Bigfoot/Sasquatch and paranormal world.

As on previous occasions, the chances of a Bigfoot encounter after loud and reckless campers, were unlikely. Yet, some of the undaunted BF hunters, made treks into the woods at night, and later joined those of us who stayed back, to gather around a campfire to be entertained by David Grant and others with their tales of previous hunts.

Don, Scott Taylor & Ron Morehead

~ 18 ~

ECETI RANCH

2016

Enlightened Contact with Extra Terrestrial Intelligence

Eryn had heard about this ranch (there are actually some yaks there) somewhere, and that there was mention of Bigfoot contact here. At the foot of Mount Adams, near Trout Lake, we had attended a BFRO Expedition several miles away and in the mountains and where I experienced several instances of BF activity. I had heard some non BFRO folks who thought Bigfoot were from alien (extraterrestrial) locations. (Hmmm…)

I had attended a couple of conferences where ET and BF aficionados came together. As Thom Powel, a 30-year teacher of Earth/Space Science and author of (*The Neighbors: A Contemporary Investigation of the Bigfoot/Sasquatch Phenomenon* (2003) – *Edges of Science* (2015) says at these conferences, (paraphrased) "You can tell the difference between Bigfoot and UFO aficionados by their dress and which side of the room they sit. One side wears camo/outdoor garb, and the other side dresses up, some in suits." Many Bigfooters don't attend these BF/UFO get-togethers because there's too much "Woo-woo" stuff they don't abide by.

We were asked to attend a viewing of a movie which explained what the ECETI Ranch was about. Unexplained lights, orbs and other phenomena emanated from Mt. Adams and nearby forests which were attributed to ETs. I waited for the part about Bigfoot ....., and unless I fell asleep, never heard or saw it. There were a couple of signs on the grounds mentioning Bigfoot, and I talked to one of the employees (volunteers) who told of an encounter, but that was it. Bummer – and the film which was made several years ago, predicted all coastal cities would be covered by water because of the weather by 2015. (Hmmm...)

At the edge of a field are plastic lounging chairs set up and facing Mt. Adams, where proponents of the nighttime orbs and lights emanating from the mountain can sit and sit and observe the ET phenomena.

We had a tent with a removable roof fly. Lying on my cot I watched the sky, while Eryn and Phoenix remained outside and claimed to see orbs weave in and out of nearby trees.

~ 19 ~

BF Afterthoughts

In Retrospect

After four years (2012-2016) of spending many days and nights in the Cascade and Olympic Mountains in search of Bigfoot, several thoughts have come to mind that need sharing to those who are interested in BF participation or those who want to disprove the existence of such a creature.

When my daughter, grandson and I started participating in our quest I had never seen a Bigfoot nor watched any of the TV shows or YouTube videos or anything else concerning Sasquatch or Bigfoot. Interestingly, my wife and I spent our 1965 honeymoon at Harrison Hot Springs in British Columbia where there were many signs and references to Sasquatch. Out of sight, out of mind was my mantra concerning this enigmatic entity. Sometime in the 70s my barber displayed a plaster cast of an enormous foot in his shop, which I dismissed as a joke, because he also had a mounted fish that moved and sang a song, and also the head of a jackalope (a jack rabbit head with antelope antlers).

My initiation into Bigfooting was due to my daughter's nighttime experience in 1977, as a ten-year-old, when we were at a family camp in the Cascade Mountains near Lake Chelan. I told her that what she thought she saw that looked like a tall, husky hairy man was probably a bear.

Her memory of her mountain experience was reawakened 32 years later when:

"I had an 'epiphany' one day while at the Olympic Game Farm in Sequim while observing grizzly bears standing up, playing and going about their bear-like business. It was the summer of 2009.

I asked one of the keepers if grizzly could get much taller and move more gracefully and if they were known to roam Eastern Washington's Cascade Range.

When she asked me why I was inquiring, I related my tale of that time back in 1977. She looked right at me and asked, seriously, if perhaps I had encountered a Sasquatch......

It struck me like a ton of bricks! I was hooked from that point on.

I tried to find all the information I could get my hands on and came across the BFRO website. It took me a couple years to be able to get on the list to attend an expedition that was local."

I've taken many classes or workshops to learn particular skills, like auto tune-up & repair, boat building, canoeing, survival, etc., so learning how to "hunt" Bigfoot was now added to a string of skills I hoped to learn. Similar to all skills, some cats have it (natural ability) and some cats don't. The 'don't's' Usually quit after one time – or even part way through.

BFRO is staffed and organized to seriously equip people who want to go to where the Bigfoot action occurs, and have skills in dealing with their BF target, or, to quote the Boy Scouts' motto: 'Be Prepared'. Attendees of BFRO Expeditions, don't just show up at some remote site at a certain time to hunt, but have to apply for permission to attend by submitting a résumé pertaining to camping/wilderness experience. In other words applicants are thoroughly vetted. The cost to join is another item to eliminate 'lookie-lou's'. Most expeditions only accept about 15 'newbies' (newcomers) and several old-timers. The expedition leaders are experienced and trained, and have to have a group (staff) of people to scout 'hot spot' locations, lead groups, teach groups, and demonstrate responsible camping practices.

I find it interesting that on many of the 'hunts' people have had sightings or other indications of BF activity. I suppose the more somebody spends time in the forests and pays attention to wilderness activity, BF sights and sounds will be noticeable. Also, there are those who seem to have a sort of animal magnetism, or what (according to an episode of *Seinfeld*) the Latvian's label *kavorka* or the lure of the animal, like the experience I had while night walking alongside a woman near Mount Adams. She was pelted with pinecones and suddenly got a sick headache and had to sit in a circle of Bigfooters until she recovered. My wife and daughter seem to have this attraction with animals, sort of love at first sight. I think Bigfoot has many and keenly developed senses and abilities that we don't have, or haven't developed. The sense of smell is used to detect everything from drugs and explosives to diseases and cadavers, in dogs – probably BF has this sensitivity as well as acuity in all the other senses we're aware of. I, on the other hand, seem to be as attractive as a bump on a log. Maybe I project a persona of – So, that's the best you have?!

The person with the most actual contact that I know of, with multiple sightings, is Col. Kevin, with Scott a close second. These guys have been game and BF hunting in the same areas so many times over a period of years, that most of the forest creatures know them by sight.

The more hunts I went on I got to know the BF bunches and hunting territories, and could observe those who understood the creatures with which they wanted to contact. Again, I say some people have the understanding, and some don't. Lots of money has been spent on electronic-types of devices in the hope of getting a picture or video of this enigmatic creature. Evidently, Bigfoot is able to sense this equipment, or has seen it set up and avoids it. I've spent countless hours driving around with heat sensing gizmos on top of a vehicle or with night vision binoculars, with absolutely no BF sightings. It's like BF uses us for entertainment. I know people who've seen them run right in front of them and seemingly disappear into thin air. Are these appearances simply to tease us? Do people seriously think the TV Bigfoot hunters with their crews are going to lure-in or stumble upon a Bigfoot?

Eryn is the only active Bigfooter of our three generation of BF hunters, as I am experiencing issues encountered in my advancing age, and Phoenix is working and going to college. But when we get together, we recall the many adventures we had in the forests and mountains in our neck of the woods of Washington State and Oregon.

Bigfooting with our family unit brought us into the presence of many interesting people we wouldn't have known otherwise. The same can be said for the variety of locations where we camped. Each area we visited was a neighborhood or territory for a variety of forest inhabitants – including *Bigfoot ~ Believe It Or Not!*

Printed in the United States
By Bookmasters